Life Cycles

A Frog's Life Cycle

by Jamie Rice

Bullfrog Books

Ideas for Parents and Teachers

Bullfrog Books let children practice reading informational text at the earliest reading levels. Repetition, familiar words, and photo labels support early readers.

Before Reading

- Discuss the cover photo. What does it tell them?
- Look at the picture glossary together. Read and discuss the words.

Read the Book

- "Walk" through the book and look at the photos. Let the child ask questions. Point out the photo labels.
- Read the book to the child, or have him or her read independently.

After Reading

- Prompt the child to think more. Ask: Frogs lay eggs in water. Can you name other animals that do this?

Bullfrog Books are published by Jump!
5357 Penn Avenue South
Minneapolis, MN 55419
www.jumplibrary.com

Library of Congress Cataloging-in-Publication Data

Names: Rice, Jamie, author.
Title: A frog's life cycle / by Jamie Rice.
Description: Bullfrog books.
Minneapolis, MN: Jump!, Inc., [2023]
Series: Life cycles | Includes index.
Audience: Ages 5–8
Identifiers: LCCN 2021048371 (print)
LCCN 2021048372 (ebook)
ISBN 9781636908342 (hardcover)
ISBN 9781636908359 (paperback)
ISBN 9781636908366 (ebook)
Subjects: LCSH: Frogs—Life cycles
Juvenile literature.
Classification: LCC QL668.E2 R526 2023 (print)
LCC QL668.E2 (ebook)
DDC 597.8/9156—dc23/eng/20211004
LC record available at
https://lccn.loc.gov/2021048371
LC ebook record available at
https://lccn.loc.gov/2021048372

Editor: Eliza Leahy
Designer: Emma Bersie

Photo Credits: Shutterstock, cover; Fablok/Shutterstock, 1; Brian Magnier/Shutterstock, 3; Birute Vijeikiene/Shutterstock, 4, 23tl; Astrid Gast/Shutterstock, 5, 22t, 23bl; Claudia Evans/Shutterstock, 6–7, 23tr; SanderMeertinsPhotography/Shutterstock, 7, 22mr, 23bm; Ken Griffiths/Shutterstock, 8; W. de Vries/Shutterstock, 9; David Chapman/Alamy, 10–11; Minden Pictures/SuperStock, 12–13, 22b, 23tm; Mary Ann McDonald/Getty, 14–15; Dorling Kindersley ltd/Alamy, 16–17; Biosphoto/SuperStock, 18; Steve Bower/Shutterstock, 19, 23br; FLPA/Alamy, 20–21; Juan Aceituno/Shutterstock, 22ml; Mirror-Images/Shutterstock, 24.

Printed in the United States of America at Corporate Graphics in North Mankato, Minnesota.

Table of Contents

Swim and Hop

A frog lays eggs in a pond.

The eggs float.

The middles are dark.

They start to move!

Tadpoles hatch.

They have long tails.

They swim and
breathe in water.

Then each tadpole grows legs. Two back legs grow first.

Then two front legs grow.

Lungs grow.
They can breathe air!
Now they are froglets.

froglet

A froglet looks like a frog. But it still has a tail.

The tail goes away.
Now it is an adult.
It hops!

Frogs eat bugs.

Their long tongues help.

Gulp!

tongue

Frogs swim in water.

Webbed feet help.

They lay eggs in water, too.
The life cycle begins again!

eggs

Life Cycle of a Frog

A frog's life cycle has four stages. Take a look!

Picture Glossary

float
To rest or move on a liquid.

froglets
Young frogs that are in the stage of growth between tadpoles and adults.

hatch
To break out of eggs.

life cycle
The series of changes each living thing goes through from birth to death.

tadpoles
Young frogs that live in water and have long tails but no legs.

webbed
Connected by a web or fold of skin.

Index

To Learn More

Finding more information is as easy as 1, 2, 3.

1. Go to www.factsurfer.com
2. Enter "afrog'slifecycle" into the search box.
3. Choose your book to see a list of websites.